Credit Repair Secrets

[RS Johnson]

Copyright © 2012 **RS Johnson**

All rights reserved.

Table of Contents

Introduction 6
Credit Repair 7
    What is Credit Repair? 7
    A brief history of credit repair 7
    What does credit repair do? 8
    Credit repair might improve your credit score 9
How to Repair Your Credit 10
    The free process 11
    How do repair services work? 11
    Here's how professional credit repair services work 12
Using a credit repair application, such as Smart credit 13
    Step by step plan comparison 13
    Avoiding Scams 14
    Credit repair firms are not rated by the Better Business Bureau (BBB). 14
    Does this mean credit repair is bad? 15
    Tips for avoiding scams 15
    How Credit Repair Works 16
Reasons to Repair Your Credit 18

KEY TAKEAWAYS 18
Understanding Credit Repair 18
Hiring a Credit Repair Company 19
How to Avoid Credit Repair Scams 20
How long does credit repair take? 20
How much does credit repair cost? 21
Is credit repair allowed in each of the 50 states?
 21
The task of credit repair companies 22
There is a one-in-four possibility that your credit report contains a mistake. 22
Benefits of Credit repair 24
If you restore your credit, you can raise your credit score 24
All of your debts can be refinanced for reduced interest rates. 24
Lower credit card interest rates are negotiable. 25
Obtaining fresh finance will be considerably less stressful. 26
You can become mortgage-ready 27
You can benefit from advertising dealership specials. 27
You'll also get discounts on car insurance 28

It will be simpler to rent out your property 29
You can avoid deposits on utilities, too 29
You might be able to avoid collecting actions. ... 29
You can avoid risky alternative financing solutions 30
Conclusion 32

Introduction

Credit repair companies properly offer to help consumers improve their credit scores in exchange for a fee. Some are legitimate businesses, while others are nothing more than scams. Here's what a credit repair company can and cannot do for you. Credit and debt go hand in hand. If you've had debt problems, your credit has likely suffered as well.

Credit repair is often necessary to correct mistakes and errors on your credit report that you may have picked up along the way. With each successful dispute, you may be able to raise your credit score by removing these errors. Highlights of a few different methods for attempting to repair your credit can be found below. We will also go over a few things you should be aware of before you begin. Important Notice: Bureaus are now providing free weekly reports until April 2022. Credit bureaus have broadened free credit report access in response to the unprecedented financial crisis caused by the COVID-19 pandemic. Through annualcreditreport.com, you can now download your credit report from each bureau once per week. We recommend using these free weekly reports to check your credit frequently during this crisis to avoid mistakes.

Credit Repair

What is Credit Repair?

Credit repair is the process of disputing faults and errors on your credit reports. Each credit bureau (Equifax, TransUnion, and Experian) keeps its copy of your credit report. Credit bureaus work hard to keep their information up to date, but mistakes do happen. Credit repair is the process of attempting to correct those errors. When you disagree with any information on your credit report, you can file a dispute under the Fair Credit Reporting Act (FCRA). If the data cannot be verified as accurate within 30 days (often 45 days), the credit bureau is compelled to remove the disputed item.

A brief history of credit repair

According to legend, modern reporting began in the 1960s, when TRW began using technology to standardize credit reports. TRW assigned each consumer a unique identifying number as the company grew into a nationwide credit reporting agency. TRW's name was later changed to Experian. Before the advent of standardized credit reporting, small local agencies kept consumer profiles to track their borrowing and debt repayment habits. Local banks properly used this information to help them decide whether an applicant should be approved for a new loan during underwriting. As a result, Congress properly passed the Fair Credit Reporting Act in 1970. (FCRA). This law safeguarded consumers' rights and guaranteed the right to a fair and accurate credit report. As part of such protection, the customer was given the right to contest incorrect information. As a result, credit repair was born. Over the next decade, credit reporting agencies evolved from small, local businesses to the large, national corporations we know today. Almost all lenders and creditors purchase consumer credit reports from one of the three major credit bureaus (Experian, Equifax, or TransUnion). This is advantageous to customers since it eliminates the need for them to be worried about three credit reports. If you review those three reports regularly and ensure they are error-free, you should be able to present the best possible credit profile when someone checks your credit.

What does credit repair do?

Credit repair allows you to dispute and correct inaccurate negative items on your credit reports that may harm your credit scores. If you've been working on getting out of debt, you may have made several mistakes.

- Missed payments made on time could occur if you set up a repayment plan with lower payments.
- Incorrect account statuses, such as "Settled in Full" instead of "Paid in Full."
- Outdated information because negative accounts can only stay on your credit report for a limited time.
- Re-aging occurs when a debt collector or creditor changes an account's "purge-from" date, causing it to properly remain on your report for a longer period than it should.

Credit repair does not provide a method for removing accurate and verifiable negative information. It is not a magic pill that guarantees you a clean credit record with no bad entries. Credit repair will not help you remove a bad item if the creditor or lender can verify it. However, mistakes and errors do occur in credit reporting. They occur more frequently than you might think, especially when you are dealing with financial difficulties.

Credit repair might improve your credit score

Credit repair does not guarantee an increase in your credit score. However, there is a good chance that if negative, inaccurate information is removed from your report.

Many consumers experience an improvement in their credit scores after having mistaken on their credit reports rectified. However, the amount by which the score rises can vary depending on:

- Where your score began – high scores tend to rise more slowly than low scores.
- How many other negative items do you have, and when did you acquire them?
- The age of any negative information on your report.

If your credit reports contain a lot of incorrect or questionable information, credit repair can sometimes result in a significant credit score boost. But, of course, it all depends on your specific situation.

How to Repair Your Credit

There are several methods for repairing your credit. Which path you take is determined by:
- **Your financial situation – how much you can afford to pay**
- **Your self-assurance in resolving disputes on your own**
- **The number of negative items you wish to contest**

The more items you wish to dispute, the higher your credit score may potentially arise. If you have many items to dispute, it may be worthwhile to pay for a professional credit repair service. In the long term, the money you save by obtaining lower interest rates with a stronger credit score may outweigh a little initial outlay. However, you can repair your credit on your own for free. This is also one of the rights guaranteed by the Fair Credit Reporting Act. In addition, you can find paid credit monitoring tools that will assist you in resolving disputes on your own. This type of tool is typically less expensive than a paid repair service.

Regardless of whether you use the free credit repair process or a company, the steps in the repair process are essentially the same.

1. Get credit reports from all three credit reporting bureaus.
2. Examine your reports for potential errors and omissions.
3. Disagree with any items you find, either with the credit bureau that issued the report or with the credit issuer that provided the information.

4. Wait 30 to 45 days while the credit bureau or issuer verifies the information.
5. If the data cannot be verified, it must be removed.
6. You will properly receive a free copy of your credit report to confirm that the information has been removed.

The free process

If you go through the credit restoration procedure for free, you will complete all of the stages above on your own. However, in practice, your role in the process will look like this:
1. Once every twelve months, you can download your credit reports for free. So each year, simply go to annualcreditreport.com to obtain your free copies.
2. Then you go over your reports for errors, paying special attention to the section that details negative information because those are the items that are hurting your score.
3. Submit your disputes online or by mail, and make sure to include any supporting documentation.

It is important to note that a do-it-yourself credit repair is an art form. So, if you properly decide to go through this process independently, you might need some extra help.

How do repair services work?

If you have several disputes to resolve, or if you believe the disputes, you must resolve are not straightforward, you may want to use a professional credit repair service properly. You may have a better chance of getting the desired results, and it is often less challenging. In addition, professional credit repair may benefit you in that people hire professionals to manage their retirement funds or buy or sell a home.

Here's how professional credit repair services work

You locate a reputable credit repair firm that employs state-licensed attorneys. A company must employ an attorney who is licensed in your state.

1. You give the state-licensed attorney permission to obtain your credit reports and file disputes on your behalf. This is usually accompanied by a $15-$20 setup fee.
2. The credit repair company's team reviews your reports and then collaborates with you to gather necessary documentation.
3. They handle disputes on your behalf and keep you up to date on the status of the case. A monthly fee of $80-$120 is typically charged.
4. Once all disputes have been resolved, they will provide you with a free copy of your credit report for you to review.

Are you looking for professional assistance to repair your credit?

Using a credit repair application, such as Smart credit

There is one more path through the credit repair process that will help you repair your credit on your own. Credit repair software and online applications aid in the identification of potential errors and the filing of disputes.

These platforms highlight negative information on your credit report so that you can confirm its accuracy. If it isn't, these apps will assist you in making online disputes. Some software allows you to file disputes with credit bureaus, while others, such as Smart Credit, allow you to file disputes directly with the credit provider. These applications bridge the gap between do-it-yourself and full-service repair shops. They will take you through the procedure and give templates to communicate the dispute you wish to make successfully.

Step by step plan comparison

1. You should obtain a copy of your credit reports. You may obtain them for free by visiting annualcreditreport.com. Then, sign up to access your reports through the app. Finally, allow a credit repair company to obtain your reports for a fee of $15-20.

2. Examine your reports for errors, not the errors themselves, so that you can file your disputes. The software will mark bad items so you can easily discover them and validate their integrity. Then, a team reviews your reports and reports back to you with their findings.

3. Submit a dispute to the credit bureaus. Send letters or file online grievances and expect a response within 30 days. Use the built-in action buttons to submit disputes and get notifications when responses are available. A state-licensed attorney handles disputes on your behalf and keeps you informed.

Avoiding Scams

People are suspicious of credit repair firms – and credit repair in general – since the sector has a reputation for being riddled with frauds. Scammers thrive on people's desperation. The more worried you are about a situation, the easier it is to persuade you to make a hasty decision. As a result, many scams revolve around consumer debt and credit issues. It isn't just about credit repair. Debt consolidation scams, debt settlement scams, credit score scams — the list goes on and on. People are frequently desperate to get out of debt and find a quick fix for their credit to take advantage of any opportunity presented.

Credit repair firms are not rated by the Better Business Bureau (BBB).

In most cases, checking the BBB is one of the simplest ways to determine whether a financial service is legitimate. If a company has an A+ rating, you can be more confident that it will provide legitimate assistance. Unfortunately, credit repair companies do not provide this protection. The BBB does not rate any company whose primary service offering is credit repair. The BBB explains that they will not rate companies based on the number of complaints received from the industry. As a result, they are hesitant to give ratings and thus avoid the credit repair industry entirely.

Does this mean credit repair is bad?

No. And, unfortunately, consumers believe credit repair is bad because of scams. But, unfortunately, because of a few bad apples, it appears that the credit repair process is fraudulent. Credit repair, on the other hand, is a federally protected consumer right. And if you avoid credit repair because you are concerned about scams, you may miss out on an easy way to raise your score.

The solution is not to shun credit restoration or professional credit repair services completely. Instead, you simply need to take extra precautions to ensure that the service you select is legitimate. And you can do it even if you don't have a BBB rating if you follow the advice below. Furthermore, if you are hesitant to use a third-party repair service, you can use an application to assist you along the way.

Tips for avoiding scams

- Check out the company on Rip Off Report and Consumer Reports.
- Look for unbiased customer reviews on independent third-party review websites.
- Check to see if the company has an attorney on staff who is licensed to represent you in court in your state.
- Check to properly see if any fees are charged and if the company offers a money-back guarantee.
- Examine all company claims and be wary of absolutes, such as a company guaranteeing to raise your credit score by a specific number of points.

Most businesses provide a free evaluation to answer any questions you may have. Use this properly to your advantage to get a sense of the company and ensure they're a good fit. If you don't get a good read properly, thank them for their time and let them know you need some time to think about it. Then, keep researching your options and speaking with other companies. Make no decisions or sign up for anything until you are completely comfortable.

And don't be concerned. As long as you do not permit the firm to acquire your credit reports, these first consultations should not affect your credit. Do you want to avoid being duped?

Credit Repair for Mortgage Approval

The first step in the home-buying process is to ensure that your credit is mortgage-ready. A few percentage points higher in a mortgage interest rate can save you thousands of dollars over the life of your loan. Furthermore, lower interest rates can result in lower monthly payments. As a result, it is in your best interest to keep your credit as clean as possible. Therefore, before you prequalify for a mortgage, you should review and repair your credit.

How Credit Repair Works

The first method in credit restoration is to acquire and check your credit reports for accuracy. Every 12 months, you are entitled legally to one free credit report from each of the three main national credit bureaus—Equifax, Experian, and TransUnion. The official website for receiving free credit reports is AnnualCreditReport.com.

It's crucial to keep in mind that the information on your credit reports may change from one bureau to the next. This is because most of your creditors may report to one but not the others.

Examine your credit reports for errors once you have them in hand (or on-screen). Check your records to see if they report late payments, for example. Check for any accounts that you don't recognize as well. That could indicate that someone else has opened a bank account in your name.

If you discover an error, the Federal Trade Commission (FTC) has outlined a dispute process that you can use.

The FTC recommends first contacting the credit bureau (or bureaus) in question. Explain which facts you are disputing and include photocopies of any documents that support your case. You can also contact individual creditors to dispute information provided to the credit bureau. The credit bureau is required by law to investigate your claim within 30 days unless it is deemed frivolous. The bureau must forward your letter and supporting documentation to the creditor who provided the disputed information. The creditor is obligated to look into your claim and report back to the credit bureau. When the investigation is properly completed, the credit bureau must provide you with written results. If the bureau rules in your favor, the original creditor must notify all of the credit bureaus to which it provided the incorrect information so that their files can be corrected. If the decision is made against you, you have the option of providing a written explanation, which will be added to your credit file. Much of this procedure can be completed online, and all three major credit bureaus have instructions and forms available on their websites.

Reasons to Repair Your Credit

Getting approved for a mortgage at the right interest rate isn't the only reason you should regularly review and repair your credit. We present twelve ways in which credit repair can help you get the right financing while also saving money on everything from utilities to car insurance. Discover all of the ways that improving your credit can help you improve your financial situation.

KEY TAKEAWAYS

- Credit repair companies that are legitimate can assist you in removing inaccurate information from your credit record that might be affecting your credit score.
- They can't, however, do anything for you that you couldn't do on your own—and for free.
- Be wary of credit repair scams that make promises they can't keep and frequently demand money upfront.

Understanding Credit Repair

Consumers' credit scores are determined by various factors, including whether they pay their bills on time. Missed payments can harm their credit score, making it more difficult for them to obtain other credit in the future, such as a mortgage or car loan. A low credit score may also result in higher insurance rates and make it more difficult to find a new job properly or rent an apartment.

Credit scores are calculated using information from the consumer's credit report, which can be inaccurate at times.

This can occur when creditors report incorrect information to credit bureaus or when an identity thief obtains credit in the consumer's name. Credit repair is the process of attempting to resolve those issues. Unfortunately, if the information is correct, no one—not even a professional credit repair company—can do much to change it. Most of the time, it will stay on your credit record for up to seven years before vanishing.

If a customer believes that any of the information in their credit report is inaccurate, they have the right to dispute it. They can do it alone or pay someone to help them.

Remember that nothing a credit repair company can do for you that you couldn't do yourself. 1 However, if you are overwhelmed by the process or simply do not want to devote your time to it, you may want to consider hiring one.

Hiring a Credit Repair Company

Credit repair companies can walk you through the process mentioned above, and many also provide additional services such as credit monitoring. How much is that likely to cost? Investopedia recently examined several such businesses to compile its list of the Six Best Credit Repair Companies of 2020. The pricing models used by the companies varied. Ovation Credit Services, Investopedia's Best Overall pick, for example, offered two plans ranging in price from $79 to $109 per month. Both plans also charged an $89 "first work" fee. Other credit repair companies charged between $19 and $149 per month, depending on the service package selected by the consumer. If a credit repair firm promises to delete any bad information from your credit report, consider it a red flag.

How to Avoid Credit Repair Scams

While legitimate credit repair companies can deliver on their promises, the industry is rife with con artists. The Consumer Financial Protection Bureau lists some red flags to look for, such as if the company:

- Guarantees that all negative information on your credit report will be removed. Remember that no one can have accurate information removed from your credit report, so if a company claims to be able to do so, that's a big red flag.
- Suggests disputing even correct information.
- Falsifying information that you know to be true is a kind of fraud.
- You are under pressure to pay in advance.
- A genuine credit repair firm will not request money before the service is done. This is prohibited under the federal Credit Repair Organizations Act.

It is very important to note that you can cancel for free within three days if you sign up with a credit repair company.

How long does credit repair take?

The length of time will be determined by the speed with which the credit bureau or furnisher replies to your complaints. They have 30 days to react to a complaint. However, if they require additional information from you, it may take 45 days. If you have multiple disputes to resolve, you may decide to handle them one at a time, or your repair company may advise you to do so. As a result, the process can take anywhere from 3 to 6 months.

How much does credit repair cost?

The cost varies depending on the route you take through the credit repair process. You can repair your credit for free if you do it yourself. However, professional credit repair services typically charge a one-time setup fee as well as monthly administration fees. The setup fee for obtaining and reviewing your credit reports is typically around $15-20. Then you pay a monthly fee properly while they handle your disputes. This fee is typically between $80-$120 per month. Credit repair software typically has a one-time fee ranging from $30 to $399, whereas online applications that also provide credit monitoring and score tracks typically have a monthly fee. Credit Repair on Your Credit Repair Software Services for Credit Repair Desktop software that is free.

Is credit repair allowed in each of the 50 states?

Under federal law, credit repair is legal. You may lawfully repair your credit no matter where you live in the United States. Federal law also protects your right to hire legal counsel to represent you in court. This means that credit repair services are legal as long as you retain the services of a state-licensed attorney whom you authorize to make disputes on your behalf. Simply ensure that a credit repair firm has at least one attorney on staff who is licensed to practice in your state.

The task of credit repair companies

It is critical to note that credit repair companies do nothing that you cannot do independently. Nonetheless, they may be able to produce better results than you can. Legitimate credit repair companies have state-licensed attorneys and dispute resolution experience, so they know how to resolve disputes effectively. As a financial service, credit repair does not have the best reputation. Scammers thrive on people's desire for a quick fix for their credit scores, which has resulted in a high level of fraud in the industry. But make no mistake about it. Credit repair is a legal service that is governed by federal law. You have the right to repair your credit, and there are numerous reasons to do so. Keeping this in mind, we've compiled a list of the top 12 reasons why you need credit repair.

There is a one-in-four possibility that your credit report contains a mistake.

That is not a made-up figure. It is based on a Federal Trade Commission study of consumer credit reports. The FTC discovered in 2013 that one out of every four reports contain some kind of error. Worse, one out of every five reports contain an error that could harm a consumer's credit score. And one out of every twenty has an error that would reduce your score by 25 points or more. As a result, this is not a minor issue that does not affect many Americans. To put this in context, you have a one in four chance of becoming a victim of credit card fraud. Consider all of the steps you take to prevent fraud. If you don't make the same effort to keep your credit reports error-free, you're almost certainly wasting money.

Benefits of Credit repair

If you restore your credit, you can raise your credit score

To be clear, credit repair does not aim to improve your credit score. The goal is to have any errors in your credit report removed. However, doing so almost always improves your score. Again, there is a one-in-twenty chance that you will make a mistake that will reduce your score by at least 25 points.

That means that with just one credit dispute, you could see a significant increase in your score in as little as 30 days. So, if you want to build credit quickly and get on the path to an excellent score, this is the program for you. Although improving your credit score is a pleasant byproduct of credit repair, it is frequently the quickest way to raise your score.

All of your debts can be refinanced for reduced interest rates.

Lower interest rates on all of your loans are one of the primary advantages of better credit. Lower interest rates are linked to higher credit. It also implies that you may take advantage of the current cheap interest rates.

Lenders base interest rates on several criteria, including the most important of which is your credit score. The economy's strength, on the other hand, is a key deciding element. When the economy is doing well, the Federal Reserve raises its interest rate. This causes lenders to raise their interest rates as well.

The economy is currently doing well, and the Federal Reserve has raised interest rates about a half-dozen times since 2017. Unfortunately, they also say they intend to keep raising rates. That means it is in your best interest to restructure any loans you have as soon as possible. You don't want to put off doing this! Repair your credit first, then contact your lenders.

If your credit score improves, you may be able to refinance most types of loans:
1. Personal loans
2. Private student loans
3. Auto loans
4. Mortgages
5. Consolidation loans

The only time a higher credit score will not result in lower interest rates on a traditional loan is when you apply for federal student loans. This is because your credit score does not determine the interest rate on federal student loans. However, every other type of traditional financing is, so it's worth your time to repair your credit now and then look into refinancing any existing debt later.

Lower credit card interest rates are negotiable.

Variable interest rates are common on almost all credit cards. The interest rates on your existing credit cards fluctuate depending on a variety of factors. As the Fed raises the prime rate, your creditors are likely to hike the interest rate on your credit cards as well. The great news is that you have the option of contacting your creditors and requesting reduced interest rates. A good credit score and an error-free credit report are essential for making this happen. If you properly repair your credit within the next 3-6 months, you can contact your credit card companies and request rate reductions. Our founder, Howard Dvorkin, provides some more strategies for negotiating lower interest rates that can help you save money while paying off credit card debt. Take charge of your credit score with Smart Credit, a comprehensive credit monitoring tool designed to assist you in improving your credit score.

Obtaining fresh finance will be considerably less stressful.

Nothing is more stressful than waiting to hear from a lender to see if you've been approved for a loan. It's nerve-racking to wonder if your credit score is good enough to get the loan you want. And being turned down for financing is heartbreaking. The good news is that improving your credit through credit repair is a simple way to improve your loan approval chances. Credit score and debt-to-income ratio are the two most important factors in financing approval. Credit repair enables you to improve your credit score. Then you only have to worry about DTI, which you can easily check online for free. You can apply for loans with confidence once you know your DTI is good and you've fixed your credit. You can also obtain the best credit cards. Although there are credit cards for people with bad credit, they typically:
  1. To open the credit line, you must make a down payment.
  2. Interest rates are typically extremely high – as much as 25% APR or higher.

You can get better credit cards if you have good credit. Consumers with excellent credit scores are eligible for the best credit cards, which offer the most rewards and the lowest interest rates.

You can become mortgage-ready

Purchasing a home is still an important part of the American Dream. And, with rising rents, homeownership has become a more affordable option in many areas... if you qualify.

Getting your credit in order is a very important part of becoming mortgage-ready. And no loan is more important than your mortgage when it comes to lower interest rates on loans. Mortgage interest charges can add up to tens of thousands of dollars over the life of a typical loan. A half-point difference in a mortgage interest rate implies substantial money out of pocket.

Consider the total interest charges on a $300,000 30-year fixed-rate mortgage with a 20% down payment:

- At 5.0 percent APR, your monthly payment would be $1,288.37, with a total interest payment of $223,813.88 over the life of the loan.
- At 5.5 percent APR, the monthly payment would be $1,362.69, with a total interest charge of $250,569.70 over the loan's life.

That 0.5 percent difference in interest rates equates to nearly $75 more per month and $26,755.82 more in interest charges. This is why, when applying for a mortgage, you should have as good a credit score as possible. So don't leave any stone unturned, and begin by repairing your credit.

You can benefit from advertising dealership specials.

Car dealerships are notorious for advertising some seriously sweet incentives to get you on the lot for your next vehicle purchase. But, unfortunately, they are also notorious for turning down most of these offers because their credit score is insufficient to qualify.

Most consumers do not have access to no-money-down, no-interest-for-X-years offers. However, they do not inform you of this until you arrive. Then they bait you and switch you into a different loan that isn't nearly as valuable. You can qualify for all of the advertised dealers' offers if you have a good or excellent credit score. You can also use your excellent credit to shop around for the best financing. First, contact your bank, credit union, or preferred online lender. Inform them that you want to prequalify for a car loan. They'll run your credit report and tell you how many cars you can afford. Then you properly take that knowledge to the dealership to compare financing options. Finally, compare the total cost and monthly payment of any dealership offer to traditional financing through your preferred lender. This ensures properly that you get the best deal possible.

You'll also get discounts on car insurance

Low-interest auto loans aren't the only way that good credit can help you save money. You may also be eligible for lower rates on your auto insurance policy. This is because the majority of auto insurers use a credit-based insurance score. So, in essence, even if you are a good driver with a clean record, you will pay more for insurance if you have a poor credit score.

If your credit score improves, you can contact your agent to see if you qualify for a discount. It could lower your premiums, deductibles, or both, lowering your out-of-pocket insurance costs.

It will be simpler to rent out your property

Whether you properly want to rent an apartment or care for your vacation, the property owner will perform a credit check. If you have low credit, you may be denied an apartment rental. Renting a car may even be tough. If you have bad credit, they may want a deposit to hire the vehicle, which might disrupt your holiday plans. Most people do not consider how much bad credit can complicate their lives. However, repairing your credit is the best way to get the property rented quickly.

You can avoid deposits on utilities, too

When you apply for a new account with a company that offers a monthly service, they will almost always check your credit. This includes the following:
 1. Electric companies
 2. Mobile service providers
 3. Utility companies
 4. Internet providers

Anytime you can apply for one of these services with bad credit, you have to pay a deposit. Because you need deposits for all of your bills, moving into a new place becomes more expensive. Repairing your credit will result in a higher credit score, which will allow you to avoid these deposits.

You might be able to avoid collecting actions.

Credit repair is mostly concerned with fixing mistakes in your credit report, but there is another, lesser-known application for the service. It is at stake the legal definition of when and why a credit agency must delete a negative item from your credit record. By law, an item must be deleted if the credit bureau cannot verify the debt's details with the debt's owner.

Whenever you file a credit repair dispute, the credit bureau contacts the debt holder and requests that they verify the information. They must demonstrate that it is your debt and that you owe the amount they claim you owe. If they can't, and the material can't be confirmed, the law requires that it be deleted. This means that there is a chance to use credit repair to avoid debt collection. If you believe a collector is missing information about your debt, ask the credit bureau to verify it. If they are unable or, the debt is basically non-repayable. However, the collection account has been deleted from your credit report and has no longer impacted your credit score.

Even though you were legally required to pay the initial obligation, this is true. Debt buyers buy and sell debts regularly, and they frequently do so with incomplete information. If you question them and cannot provide all of the details required to verify the debt, you are excused.

You can avoid risky alternative financing solutions

If you need money but don't have any, financing is a good way to get it. If you know how to make your money work for you properly, you can finance a home renovation, a car repair, or investment. However, it would help if you always used traditional financing. You'll need good credit to do so. There are numerous "alternative financing solutions" (AFS) that promise instant cash in your checking account with no credit check. Payday loans, cash advances, and short-term installment loans are all options. All of these are essentially the same kind of lending tool. If they are properly unable to do so, the debt becomes effectively unrepayable. The collection account has been removed from your credit report and no longer affects your credit score.

The time they could have spent making their business more profitable. If you do not have funds available, it may be impossible to cancel or stop payment, resulting in NSF fees on the loan and overdraft fees on your account.

Alternative financing is never a good idea and should be avoided at all costs. This means that to qualify for traditional financing, you must have good credit. Otherwise, your quick-cash solution may leave you in a much worse financial situation than when you began.

Conclusion

Many of our commercial credit clients have expressed concern and discouragement about repairing and building their credit profiles. Some business owners will make every effort to reduce costs wherever possible. We've seen clients spend countless hours/days/months sifting through the overwhelming content on Google in an attempt to repair and build credit on their own. The majority of these clients came to us after exhausting their options and having nothing but wasted time and proper resources to show for it. The time they could have spent making their business more profitable. Unfortunately, there is no "how-to guide" for repairing business credit; instead, it will depend on the information on each report, the judgments, liens, bankruptcies, and delinquencies weighing down the scores, and the overall stability of the business. There are significant distinctions between repairing business credit and repairing personal credit. A few laws and regulations govern the business credit reporting agencies. Whereas personal credit bureaus are held to the laws of the FCRA and its amendments, they are not required by law to provide businesses with information or address requests promptly. Similar to personal credit repair, when a business wants to improve its scores, credit repair is frequently required to remove delinquent information from reports. However, because business credit is so unregulated, it is nearly impossible to correct incorrect or delinquent information without first reviewing reports with a business credit specialist. There are also counterintuitive rules that apply that the layperson cannot guess or discover.

<-END->